POETRY FOR SUPPER

POETRY
FOR SUPPER

*

R. S. THOMAS

1961
DUFOUR EDITIONS
CHESTER SPRINGS

© R. S. Thomas 1958
First published, 1958
Second impression, 1961

Library of Congress Catalog Card
Number 61-14094

Printed in Great Britain by Butler & Tanner Ltd., Frome and London

FOR
JOHN BETJEMAN
AND
RUPERT HART-DAVIS

CONTENTS

BORDER BLUES 9

TEMPTATION OF A POET 14

EVANS 15

ON HEARING A WELSHMAN SPEAK 16

CHAPEL DEACON 17

A DAY IN AUTUMN 18

GREEN CATEGORIES 19

LOWRI DAFYDD 20

AGE 21

SAILOR POET 22

THE MUCK FARMER 23

WINTER 24

THE CAT AND THE SEA 25

THE LETTER 26

THE VIEW FROM THE WINDOW 27

THE COUNTRY CLERGY 28

AP HUW'S TESTAMENT 29

THE JOURNEY 30

DEATH OF A POET 31

FABLE 32

A BLACKBIRD SINGING 33

POETRY FOR SUPPER 34

A GARDENER 35

IAGO PRYTHERCH 36

POWER 37

ON A LINE IN SANDBURG 38

MEET THE FAMILY 39

COMPOSITION 40

THE CURE   41

EXPATRIATES   42

PHOBIA   43

ABSOLUTION   44

THE CRY   45

BREAD   46

FARM WIFE   47

EPITAPH   48

BORDER BLUES

All along the border the winds blow
Eastward from Wales, and the rivers flow
Eastward from Wales with the roads and the railways,
Reversing the path of the old migrations.
And the winds say, It is April, bringing scents
Of dead heroes and dead saints.
But the rivers are surly with brown water
Running amok, and the men to tame them
Are walking the streets of a far town.

Spring is here and the birds are singing;
Spring is here and the bells are ringing
In country churches, but not for a bride.
The sexton breaks the unleavened earth
Over the grave.
                Are there none to marry?
There is still an Olwen teasing a smile
Of bright flowers out of the grass,
Olwen in nylons. Quick, quick,
Marry her someone. But Arthur leers
And turns again to the cramped kitchen
Where the old mother sits with her sons and daughters
At the round table. Ysbaddaden Penkawr's
Cunning was childish measured with hers.

*

I was going up the road and Beuno beside me
Talking in Latin and old Welsh,
When a volley of voices struck us; I turned,
But Beuno had vanished, and in his place
There stood the ladies from the council houses:

Blue eyes and Birmingham yellow
Hair, and the ritual murder of vowels.
Excuse me, I said, I have an appointment
On the high moors; it's the first of May
And I must go the way of my fathers
Despite the loneli—you might say rudeness.

Sheep song round me in the strong light;
The ancient traffic of glad birds
Returning to breed in the green sphagnum—
What am I doing up here alone
But paying homage to a bleak, stone
Monument to an evicted people?
Go back, go back; from the rough heather
The grouse repels me, and with slow step
I turn to go, but down not back.

*

Eryr Pengwern, penngarn llwyt heno . . .
We still come in by the Welsh gate, but it's along way
To Shrewsbury now from the Welsh border.
There's the train, of course, but I like the 'buses;
We go each Christmas to the pantomime:
It was 'The Babes' this year, all about nature.
On the way back, when we reached the hills—
All black they were with a trimming of stars—
Some of the old ones got sentimental,
Singing Pantycelyn; but we soon drowned them;
It's funny, these new tunes are easy to learn.
We reached home at last, but *diawl!* I was tired.
And to think that my grand-dad walked it each year,
Scythe on shoulder to mow the hay,
And his own waiting when he got back.

*

Mi sydd fachgen ifanc, ffôl,
Yn byw yn ôl fy ffansi.
Riding on a tractor,
Whistling tunes
From the world's dance-halls;
Dreaming of the girl, Ceridwen,
With the red lips,
And red nails.
Coming in late,
Rising early
To flog the carcase
Of the brute earth;
A lad of the 'fifties,
Gay, tough,
I sit, as my fathers have done,
In the back pews on Sundays
And have fun.

★

Going by the long way round the hedges;
Speaking to no one, looking north
At every corner, she comes from the wise man.
Five lengths of yarn from palm to elbow
Wound round the throat, then measured again
Till the yarn shrinks, a cure for jaundice.

Hush, not a word. When we've finished milking
And the stars are quiet, we'll get out the car
And go to Llangurig; the mare's bewitched
Down in the pasture, letting feg
Tarnish the mirror of bright grass.

★

Six drops in a bottle,
And an old rhyme
Scratched on a slate
With stone pencil:
Abracadabra,
Count three, count nine;
Bury it in your neighbour's field
At bed-time.

*

As I was saying, I don't hold with war
Myself, but when you join your unit
Send me some of your brass buttons
And I'll have a shot at the old hare
In the top meadow, for the black cow
Is a pint short each morning now.

Be careful, mind where you're going.
These headlights dazzle, their bright blade
Reaps us a rich harvest of shadow.
But when they have gone, it is darker still,
And the vixen moves under the hill
With a new boldness, fretting her lust
To rawness on the unchristened grass.
It's easy to stray from the main road
And find yourself at the old *domen*.
I once heard footsteps in the leaves,
And saw men hiding behind the trunks
Of the trees. I never went there again,
Though that was at night, and the night is different.

The day divides us, but at night
We meet in the inn and warm our hearts
At the red beer with yarn and song;
Despite our speech we are not English,
And our wit is sharp as an axe yet,
Finding the bone beneath the skin
And the soft marrow in the bone.
We are not English . . . *Ni bydd diwedd*
Byth ar sŵn y delyn aur.
Though the strings are broken, and time sets
The barbed wire in their place,
The tune endures; on the cracked screen
Of life our shadows are large still
In history's fierce afterglow.

TEMPTATION OF A POET

The temptation is to go back,
To make tryst with the pale ghost
Of an earlier self, to summon
To the mind's hearth, as I would now,
You, Prytherch, there to renew
The lost poetry of our talk
Over the embers of that world
We built together; not built either,
But found lingering on the farm
As sun lingers about the corn
That in the stackyard makes its own light.

And if I yield and you come
As in the old days with nature's
Lore green on your tongue,
Your coat a sack, pinned at the corners
With the rain's drops, could the talk begin
Where it left off? Have I not been
Too long away? There is a flaw
In your first premise, or else the mind's
Acid sours the soft light
That charmed me.

              Prytherch, I am undone;
The past calls with the cool smell
Of autumn leaves, but the mind draws
Me onward blind with the world's dust,
Seeking a spring that my heart fumbles.

EVANS

Evans? Yes, many a time
I came down his bare flight
Of stairs into the gaunt kitchen
With its wood fire, where crickets sang
Accompaniment to the black kettle's
Whine, and so into the cold
Dark to smother in the thick tide
Of night that drifted about the walls
Of his stark farm on the hill ridge.

It was not the dark filling my eyes
And mouth appalled me; not even the drip
Of rain like blood from the one tree
Weather-tortured. It was the dark
Silting the veins of that sick man
I left stranded upon the vast
And lonely shore of his bleak bed.

And as he speaks time turns,
The swift years revolve
Backwards. There Goronwy comes
Again to his own shore.
Now in a mountain parish
The words leave the Book
To swarm in the honeyed mind
Of Morgan. Glyn Dŵr stands
And sees the flames fall back
Like waves from the charred timbers
Before taking his place
Behind the harp's slack bars
From which the singer called him.
Look, in this resinous church,
As the long prayers are wound
Once more on the priest's tongue,
Dafydd reproves his eyes'
Impetuous falconry
About the kneeling girl.
Stones to the walls fly back,
The gay manors are full
Of music; the poets return
To feed at the royal tables.
Who dreams of failure now
That the oak woods are loud
With the last hurrying feet
Seeking the English plain?

CHAPEL DEACON

Who put that crease in your soul,
Davies, ready this fine morning
For the staid chapel, where the Book's frown
Sobers the sunlight? Who taught you to pray
And scheme at once, your eyes turning
Skyward, while your swift mind weighs
Your heifer's chances in the next town's
Fair on Thursday? Are your heart's coals
Kindled for God, or is the burning
Of your lean cheeks because you sit
Too near that girl's smouldering gaze?
Tell me, Davies, for the faint breeze
From heaven freshens and I roll in it,
Who taught you your deft poise?

A DAY IN AUTUMN

It will not always be like this,
The air windless, a few last
Leaves adding their decoration
To the trees' shoulders, braiding the cuffs
Of the boughs with gold; a bird preening
In the lawn's mirror. Having looked up
From the day's chores, pause a minute,
Let the mind take its photograph
Of the bright scene, something to wear
Against the heart in the long cold.

GREEN CATEGORIES

You never heard of Kant, did you, Prytherch?
A strange man! What would he have said
Of your life here, free from the remote
War of antinomies; free also
From mind's uncertainty faced with a world
Of its own making?
                                    Here all is sure;
Things exist rooted in the flesh,
Stone, tree and flower. Even while you sleep
In your low room, the dark moor exerts
Its pressure on the timbers. Space and time
Are not the mathematics that your will
Imposes, but a green calendar
Your heart observes; how else could you
Find your way home or know when to die
With the slow patience of the men who raised
This landmark in the moor's deep tides?

His logic would have failed; your mind, too,
Exposed suddenly to the cold wind
Of genius, faltered. Yet at night together
In your small garden, fenced from the wild moor's
Constant aggression, you could have been at one,
Sharing your faith over a star's blue fire.

LOWRI DAFYDD

My name is Lowri Dafydd;
Famous for nursing I was.
I rode pillion on a winged horse
Through the high passes of cloud
To come to a queen's palace.
Airy fingers undid the knot
In time's stubborn bandage
About my green eyes.
Who knows how long I stayed?
My pay was the sweet talk
In sun-dusted rooms
Of folk, busy as flowers,
Praising my hands' skill.
When I returned, stars were out
Over my roof, the door fallen
About its hinges, and on the hearth
A cold wind blowing for ever.

AGE

Farmer, you were young once.
And she was there, waiting, the unique flower
That only you could find in the wild moor
Of your experience.
Gathered, she grew to the warm woman
Your hands had imagined
Fondling soil in the spring fields.

And she was fertile; four strong sons
Stood up like corn in June about you.
But, farmer, did you cherish, tend her
As your own flesh, this dry stalk
Where the past murmurs its sad tune?
Is this the harvest of your blithe sowing?

If you had spared from your long store
Of days lavished upon the land
But one for her where she lay fallow,
Drying, hardening, withering to waste.
But now—too late! You're an old tree,
Your roots groping in her in vain.

SAILOR POET

His first ship; his last poem;
And between them what turbulent acres
Of sea or land with always the flesh ebbing
In slow waves over the salt bones.

But don't be too hard; so to have written
Even in smoke on such fierce skies,
Or to have brought one poem safely to harbour
From such horizons is not now to be scorned.

THE MUCK FARMER

This man swaying dully before us
Is a muck farmer, to use his own words;
A man unfit to breed the sleek herds,
That win prizes and give the thick milk,
White as the teeth it builds. His rare smile,
Cracked as the windows of his stone house
Sagging under its weight of moss,
Falls on us palely like the wan moon
That cannot pierce the thin cloud
Of March. His speech is a rank garden,
Where thought is choked in the wild tangle
Of vain phrases.
                  Leave him, then, crazed and alone
To pleach his dreams with his rough hands.
Our ways have crossed and tend now apart;
Ours to end in a field wisely sown,
His in the mixen of his warped heart.

WINTER

Too cold for love and the white angels
Of snow that kept their calm vigil
On gentler nights; only a voice
Shrill as the blood in our thin veins.

It was the voice of the sea wind
Blown through the wood's darkness, we heard it
Not with our ears but our hearts declining
With slow insistence the word 'grief'.
Not the sound of the wind urging
The sea horses up the remote shore
Rough with salt, but the wind bruising
Invisible knuckles upon the boughs
Of the bare trees, rigid with frost.

I said fiercely—it was the stars' breath
Whitening your hair—Let the wind speak
For us also, opening an old wound
That time dealt us; let the night fill
With sharp music, nature and man
At one a moment in their pain.

THE CAT AND THE SEA

It is a matter of a black cat
On a bare cliff top in March
Whose eyes anticipate
The gorse petals;

The formal equation of
A domestic purr
With the cold interiors
Of the sea's mirror.

THE LETTER

And to be able to put at the end
Of the letter Athens, Florence—some name
That the spirit recalls from earlier journeys
Through the dark wood, seeking the path
To the bright mansions; cities and towns
Where the soul added depth to its stature.

And not to worry about the date,
The words being timeless, concerned with truth,
Beauty, love, misery even,
Which has its seasons in the long growth
From seed to flesh, flesh to spirit.

And laying aside the pen, dipped
Not in tears' volatile liquid
But in black ink of the heart's well,
To read again what the hand has written
To the many voices' quiet dictation.

THE VIEW FROM THE WINDOW

Like a painting it is set before one,
But less brittle, ageless; these colours
Are renewed daily with variations
Of light and distance that no painter
Achieves or suggests. Then there is movement,
Change, as slowly the cloud bruises
Are healed by sunlight, or snow caps
A black mood; but gold at evening
To cheer the heart. All through history
The great brush has not rested,
Nor the paint dried; yet what eye,
Looking coolly, or, as we now,
Through the tears' lenses, ever saw
This work and it was not finished?

THE COUNTRY CLERGY

I see them working in old rectories
By the sun's light, by candlelight,
Venerable men, their black cloth
A little dusty, a little green
With holy mildew. And yet their skulls,
Ripening over so many prayers,
Toppled into the same grave
With oafs and yokels. They left no books,
Memorial to their lonely thought
In grey parishes; rather they wrote
On men's hearts and in the minds
Of young children sublime words
Too soon forgotten. God in his time
Or out of time will correct this.

AP HUW'S TESTAMENT

There are four verses to put down
For the four people in my life,
Father, mother, wife

And the one child. Let me begin
With her of the immaculate brow
My wife; she loves me. I know how.

My mother gave me the breast's milk
Generously, but grew mean after,
Envying me my detached laughter.

My father was a passionate man,
Wrecked after leaving the sea
In her love's shallows. He grieves in me.

What shall I say of my boy,
Tall, fair? He is young yet;
Keep his feet free of the world's net.

THE JOURNEY

And if you go up that way, you will meet with a man,
Leading a horse, whose eyes declare:
There is no God. Take no notice.
There will be other roads and other men
With the same creed, whose lips yet utter
Friendlier greeting, men who have learned
To pack a little of the sun's light
In their cold eyes, whose hands are waiting
For your hand. But do not linger.
A smile is payment; the road runs on
With many turnings towards the tall
Tree to which the believer is nailed.

DEATH OF A POET

Laid now on his smooth bed
For the last time, watching dully
Through heavy eyelids the day's colour
Widow the sky, what can he say
Worthy of record, the books all open,
Pens ready, the faces, sad,
Waiting gravely for the tired lips
To move once—what can he say?

His tongue wrestles to force one word
Past the thick phlegm; no speech, no phrases
For the day's news, just the one word 'sorry';
Sorry for the lies, for the long failure
In the poet's war; that he preferred
The easier rhythms of the heart
To the mind's scansion; that now he dies
Intestate, having nothing to leave
But a few songs, cold as stones
In the thin hands that asked for bread.

FABLE

It was the last day of the world,
The green flames all burning low;
The buds swarming for the last time
In boughs over the earth's hive.

The spent lovers, too bored to kiss,
Watched each other across the sand,
The dry bed never to be remade
With cool tides by the moon's hand.

A BLACKBIRD SINGING

It seems wrong that out of this bird,
Black, bold, a suggestion of dark
Places about it, there yet should come
Such rich music, as though the notes'
Ore were changed to a rare metal
At one touch of that bright bill

You have heard it often, alone at your desk
In a green April, your mind drawn
Away from its work by sweet disturbance
Of the mild evening outside your room.

A slow singer, but loading each phrase
With history's overtones, love, joy
And grief learned by his dark tribe
In other orchards and passed on
Instinctively as they are now,
But fresh always with new tears.

'Listen, now, verse should be as natural
As the small tuber that feeds on muck
And grows slowly from obtuse soil
To the white flower of immortal beauty.'

'Natural, hell! What was it Chaucer
Said once about the long toil
That goes like blood to the poem's making?
Leave it to nature and the verse sprawls,
Limp as bindweed, if it break at all
Life's iron crust. Man, you must sweat
And rhyme your guts taut, if you'd build
Your verse a ladder.'
                        'You speak as though
No sunlight ever surprised the mind
Groping on its cloudy path.'

'Sunlight's a thing that needs a window
Before it enter a dark room.
Windows don't happen.'
                      So two old poets,
Hunched at their beer in the low haze
Of an inn parlour, while the talk ran
Noisily by them, glib with prose.

A GARDENER

Digging
Day after day
With bent back
And huge, raw hands,
Scalded with cold.

And sickness within,
The corrosive ulcer
Gnawing the frame,
Strong axled
With thew and bone.

But the eyes blue;
The boreal flame
Of the spirit steady,
And laughter crackling
At the good joke.

IAGO PRYTHERCH

Iago Prytherch, forgive my naming you.
You are so far in your small fields
From the world's eye, sharpening your blade
On a cloud's edge, no one will tell you
How I made fun of you, or pitied either
Your long soliloquies, crouched at your slow
And patient surgery under the faint
November rays of the sun's lamp.

Made fun of you? That was their graceless
Accusation, because I took
Your rags for theme, because I showed them
Your thought's bareness; science and art,
The mind's furniture, having no chance
To install themselves, because of the great
Draught of nature sweeping the skull.

Fun? Pity? No word can describe
My true feelings. I passed and saw you
Labouring there, your dark figure
Marring the simple geometry
Of the square fields with its gaunt question.
My poems were made in its long shadow
Falling coldly across the page.

POWER

Power, farmer? It was always yours.
Not the new physics' terrible threat
To the world's axle, nor the mind's subtler
Manipulation of our debt

To nature; but an old gift
For weathering the slow recoil
Of empires with a tree's patience,
Rooted in the dark soil.

ON A LINE IN SANDBURG

'Where did the blood come from?
Before I bit, before I sucked
The red meat, the blood was there
Nourishing sweetly the roots of hair.'

'The blood came from your mother
By way of the long gut-cord;
You were the pain in her side;
You were born on a blood-dark tide.'

'My mother also was young
Once, but her cheeks were red
Even then. From its hidden source
The hot blood ran on its old course.

Where did the blood come from?'

MEET THE FAMILY

John One takes his place at the table,
He is the first part of the fable;
His eyes are dry as a dead leaf.
Look on him and learn grief.

John Two stands in the door
Dumb; you have seen that face before
Leaning out of the dark past,
Tortured in thought's bitter blast.

John Three is still outside
Drooling where the daylight died
On the wet stones; his hands are crossed
In mourning for a playmate lost.

John All and his lean wife,
Whose forced complicity gave life
To each loathed foetus, stare from the wall,
Dead not absent. The night falls.

COMPOSITION

He never could decide what to write
About, knowing only that his pen
Must not rust in the stale tears of men
Too long dead, nor yet take to flight
Before measuring the thought's height
Above the earth, whose green thoroughfares,
Though hedged thickly with the heart's cares,
Still let in the sun's natural light.

He tried truth; but the pen's scalpel tip
Was too sharp; thinly the blood ran
From unseen wounds, but too red to dip
Again in, so, back where he began,
He tried love; slowly the blood congealed
Like dark flowers saddening a field.

THE CURE

But what to do? Doctors in verse
Being scarce now, most poets
Are their own patients, compelled to treat
Themselves first; their complaint being
Peculiar always. Consider, you,
Whose rough hands manipulate
The fine bones of a sick culture,
What areas of that infirm body
Depend solely on a poet's cure.

EXPATRIATES

Not British; certainly
Not English. Welsh
With all the associations,
Black hair and black heart
Under a smooth skin,
Sallow as vellum; sharp
Of bone and wit that is turned
As a knife against us.
Four centuries now
We have been leaving
The hills and the high moors
For the jewelled pavements
Easing our veins of their dark peat
By slow transfusions.
In the drab streets
That never knew
The cold stream's sibilants
Our tongues are coated with
A dustier speech.
With the year's passing
We have forgotten
The far lakes,
Aled and Eiddwen, whose blue litmus
Alone could detect
The mind's acid.

PHOBIA

This poor woman who was afraid,
Afraid of the gestures the trees made
In the wood at night or on the blind
At home; afraid of the heart's sound,
The intestinal rumour, the ripe swell
Of muscles under the taut skin;
Through long brooding conceived at last
Peculiar sickness, nurtured it
And reared it, till it was of age
To practise incest with its mother.
From such foul intercourse death came
Bloodily forth.
              Take her cold hand,
Spirit, and lead her gently away
From the mind's darkness into the light,
If not the comfort, of truth's flame.

ABSOLUTION

Prytherch, man, can you forgive
From your stone altar on which the light's
Bread is broken at dusk and dawn
One who strafed you with thin scorn
From the cheap gallery of his mind?
It was you who were right the whole time;
Right in this that the day's end
Finds you still in the same field
In which you started, your soul made strong
By the earth's incense, the wind's song.
While I have worn my soul bare
On the world's roads, seeking what lay
Too close for the mind's lenses to see,
And come now with the first stars
Big on my lids westward to find
With the slow lifting up of your hand
No welcome, only forgiveness.

THE CRY

Don't think it was all hate
That grew there; love grew there, too,
Climbing by small tendrils where
The warmth fell from the eyes' blue

Flame. Don't think even the dirt
And the brute ugliness reigned
Unchallenged. Among the fields
Sometimes the spirit, enchained

So long by the gross flesh, raised
Suddenly there its wild note of praise.

BREAD

Hunger was loneliness, betrayed
By the pitiless candour of the stars'
Talk, in an old byre he prayed

Not for food; to pray was to know
Waking from a dark dream to find
The white loaf on the white snow;

Not for warmth, warmth brought the rain's
Blurring of the essential point
Of ice probing his raw pain.

He prayed for love, love that would share
His rags' secret; rising he broke
Like sun crumbling the gold air

The live bread for the starved folk.

FARM WIFE

Hers is the clean apron, good for fire
Or lamp to embroider, as we talk slowly
In the long kitchen, while the white dough
Turns to pastry in the great oven,
Sweetly and surely as hay making
In a June meadow; hers are the hands,
Humble with milking, but still now
In her wide lap as though they heard
A quiet music, hers being the voice
That coaxes time back to the shadows
In the room's corners. O, hers is all
This strong body, the safe island
Where men may come, sons and lovers,
Daring the cold seas of her eyes.

EPITAPH

The poem in the rock and
The poem in the mind
Are not one.
It was in dying
I tried to make them so.